OPTICAL ILLUSIONS

D0028856

Publications International, Ltd.

Puzzle creators: Cihan Altay, Barry Clarke, Grabarchuk Family, Robin Humer, Gianni Sarcone, Shavan R. Spears, Jen Torche

Puzzle illustrators: Helem An, Robin Humer, Shavan R. Spears, Jen Torche

Additional puzzle art: Cynthia Fliege, Shutterstock.com

Louis Weber, CEO
Publications International, Ltd.
8140 Lehigh Avenue
Morton Grove, IL 60053

ISBN: 978-1-68022-776-5

Manufactured in U.S.A.

8 7 6 5 4 3 2 1

SEEING IS DECEIVING!

For all of the complex and captivating things scientists have discovered, the human brain is still the most mysterious part of our bodies. One thing we do know is that the brain's interpretation of the world isn't always literal. When it comes to perception, our brain is good at filling in the gaps and drawing visual conclusions that may not match reality.

Living in our 3-dimensional world, we are constantly bombarded by common everyday optical illusions. In an effort to keep our surroundings familiar and understandable, the brain takes a few liberties. For the most part, we never notice what we are missing. In short, we oftentimes see what we want to see.

It's no wonder that optical illusions are so fascinating! They have, after all, been around for centuries and used for a number of purposes: psychological exams, creative advertisements, and just plain fun! Over the years, they've also been employed as educational tools. In order to decipher a typical illusion, our brain must function in ways it isn't accustomed to. Stepping outside our comfort zone and thinking in ways that are creative and challenging to our visual perception is precisely kind of brain exercise we need.

So don't be mistaken about the illusions in this book—they do much more than play with how we see the world. They are designed to get our cognitive motors in gear, our perception heightened, and our concentration razor sharp. And, most importantly, they're a lot of fun!

UP IN THE AIR

You won't find this construction floating in the air—or anywhere! It's an impossible structure that cannot exist in 3 dimensions.

HIDDEN ELEPHANT

The elephant below seems to have shape, but it's only an illusion. By readjusting some lines, it appears that an elephant has risen out of the background.

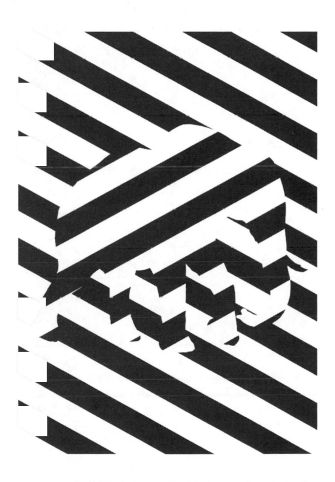

WARPED STRAW

Illusions aren't just tricks of perception. Sometimes, science is involved. This straw is warped due to what's known as refraction, a property that causes light to bend. Because of the differences in density between the straw in the water and the straw outside the water, light bends it in different ways, causing a warped appearance.

BLOCK PARTY

These blocks are static on the page, but that doesn't stop them from appearing to spin around.

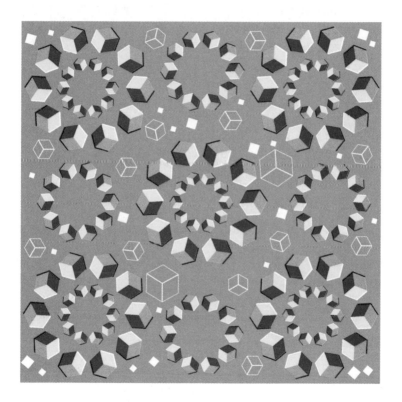

BLIVET

This blivet, or trident, is an impossible shape because it could only exist in 2 dimensions. The blivet appears to have 3 cylindrical prongs at one end and 2 rectangular prongs at the other end.

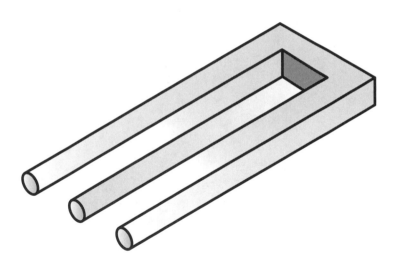

UPSTAIRS DOWNSTAIRS

Climbing upstairs or downstairs won't get you anywhere. This is another impossible structure.

DRIFTING DOTS

Let your eyes roam around this illusion and the red
dots will appear to drift. This is known as "anomalous
motion," a term used to define the appearance of
motion in a static image. Color contrasts and eye
movement contribute to relative motion effects.

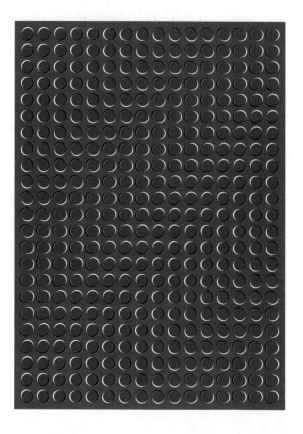

UNBUILDABLE

How would you go about building this structure? You wouldn't get far—this configuration is unbuildable.

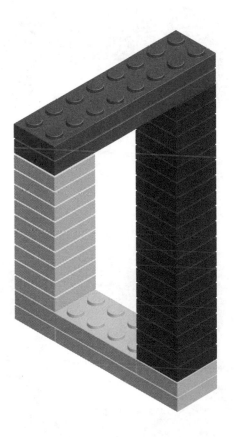

TAROT CARD SKULL

Do you see a skull or 2 girls? Like many illusions, there is more than one way to view this ambiguous image.

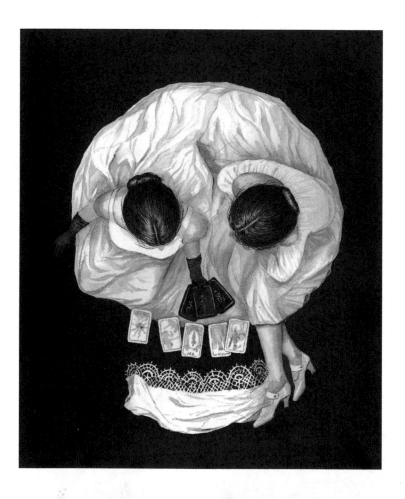

BURSTING COLORS

These waves of color seem to magically burst off the page, but it's just an illusion.

PARALLEL DIAGONALS?

In the image below, the long diagonal lines don't appear to be parallel due to the opposing directions of the short hatch marks they intersect. But as you can see in the image on the next page, the diagonal lines are parallel.

ENDLESS CLIMB

Reaching the top of this staircase is impossible. No matter how long he climbs, he will never get anywhere on this endless loop of stairs.

HANDS DRAWING HANDS

There's something strange about this image—mainly that the hands are drawing each other.

SKULL SHIFT

Though static on the page, these rows of skulls seem to shift from side to side.

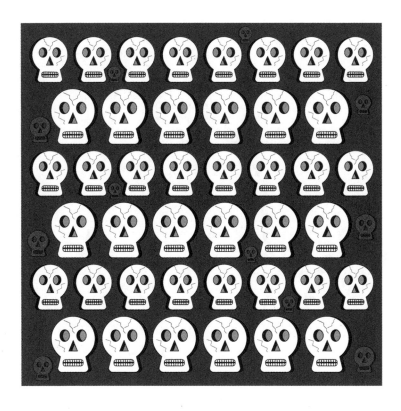

UNUSUAL PROFILE

This image was altered to create an unusual profile.

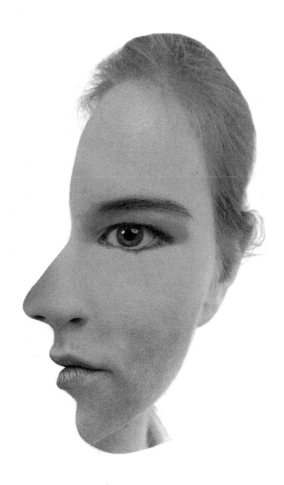

IMPOSSIBLE ENGINE

This steampunk engine and boiler could never exist in our 3-D world.

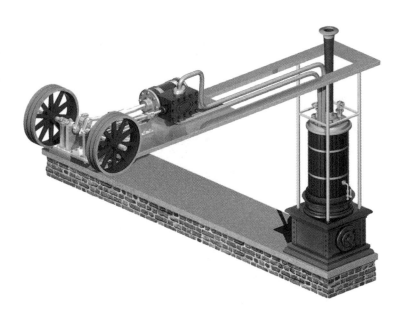

WHIRLING QUESTIONS

Do these question marks appear to whirl around?

DOMINOES

You won't find this arrangement of dominoes anywhere in the real world.

VERTICAL OR HORIZONTAL?

Which is the longer pencil—the vertical pencil or the horizontal pencil? Turn to the next page to find out.

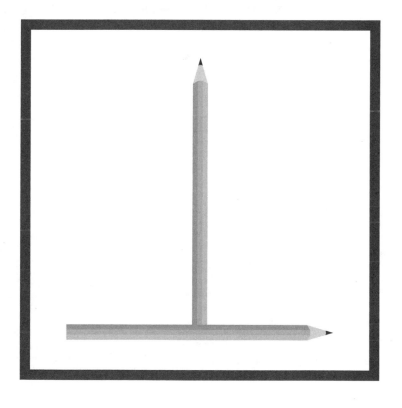

Answer on page 24.

VERTICAL OR HORIZONTAL?

While the vertical pencil looks longer, you can see here that the pencils are the same length.

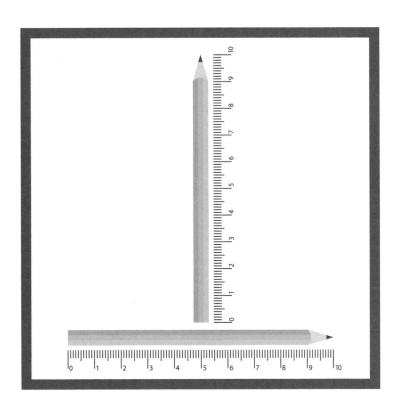

WELDED CUBE

This welded cube looks convincing at first sight, but closer inspection reveals its flaws.

CIRCULAR SURPRISE

By changing the direction of some straight lines, a circular pattern has emerged. The circular pattern seems to hover above the vertical lines in the background.

GRID ILLUSION

As you stare at this grid, do you notice the yellow dots at the intersections of red lines flash and change color?

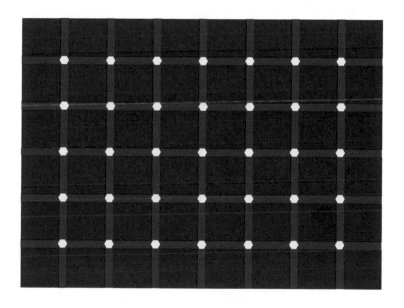

STAIRCASE TO NOWHERE

This staircase doesn't lead anywhere—except to the same level.

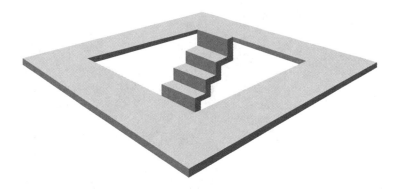

ARROW ROLLERS

Stare at these arrows and you will probably see 3 vertical columns that roll back and forth.

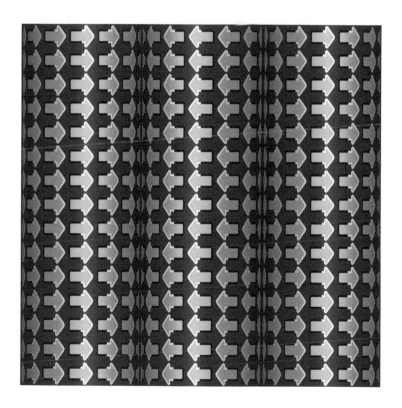

DON'T BE A PAWN

Which is the darker chesspiece in the image below? The chesspiece on the right seems darker because it is contrasted with a lighter background, but you can see on the next page that both chesspieces are the same color.

DEN OF SERPENTS

Don't be fooled by this illusion. These serpents seem to slither around, but they're really stuck on the page.

WOOD TRIANGLE

Even the best woodworker would be unable to build this impossible triangle.

CIRCLE DISTORTION

The circle placed on the triangle seems distorted, while the circle below seems fine. But both are perfect circles and are identical in size and shape.

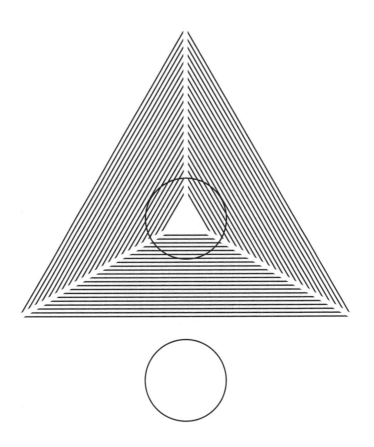

CRAZY WAVES

Ride the waves as these curved lines give the impression of peaks and valleys. Which are the peaks and which are the valleys? It all depends on your perspective!

IMPOSSIBLE POOL

There's something puzzling about this pool. It's another
impossible structure that can only exist in 2 dimensions.

ARCH RIVALS

Which is the larger arch—the black arch or white arch?
Turn to the next page to find out.

Answer on page 38.

ARCH RIVALS

At first glance, the white arch seems larger. But as you can see here, both arches are the same size.

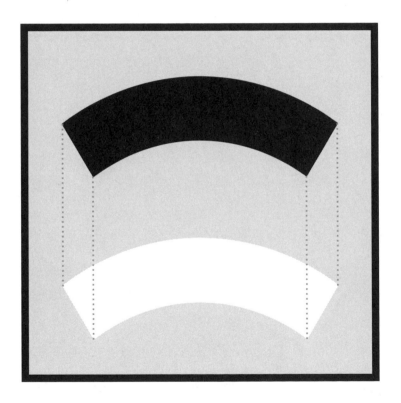

DOG'S VASE

What do you see—2 dogs or a vase? This variation on
the classic Rubin's vase illusion can be perceived as
either a vase or as 2 dogs facing each other.

STAR POWER

These stars seem to have the power to spin, but they're actually stationary on the page.

TAKE A SEAT

Taking a seat on this bench would be impossible!

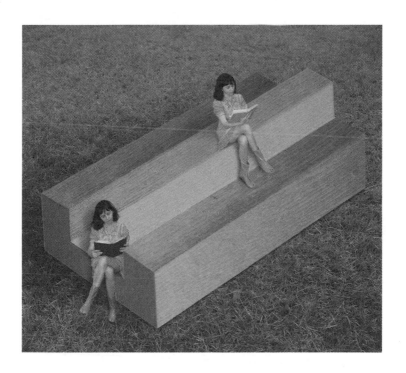

LINE LENGTHS

Are the 2 vertical lines on this page the same length?
Even though the vertical line on the left seems longer,
you can see on the next page that the vertical lines are
equal in length.

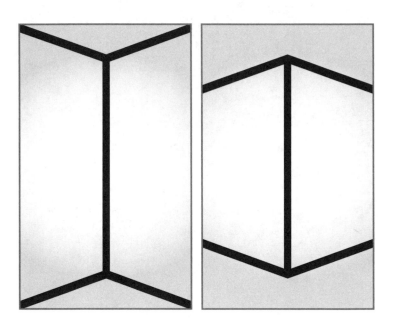

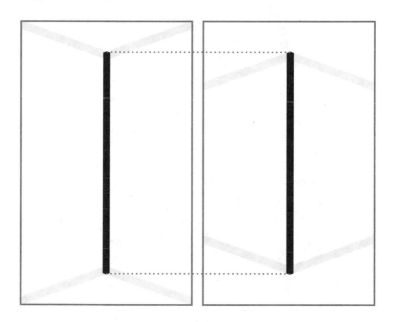

FRASER SPIRAL

In the Fraser spiral illusion, also known as the twisted cord illusion, or false spiral illusion, overlapping arc segments appear to form a spiral, but the arcs are a series of concentric circles.

MIRROR MIRROR

A framed circular mirror was used to create this illusion.

STEEL STRUCTURE

Take a look at this structure. Seems okay, right? It may look correct at a glance, but this structure couldn't be created, other than on paper.

PENCIL PUZZLER

Which completes the pencil, B or C? Turn to the next page to find out.

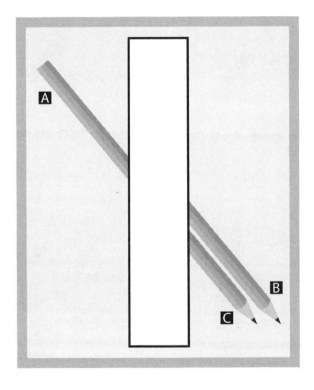

Answer on page 48.

PENCIL PUZZLER

C completes the pencil.

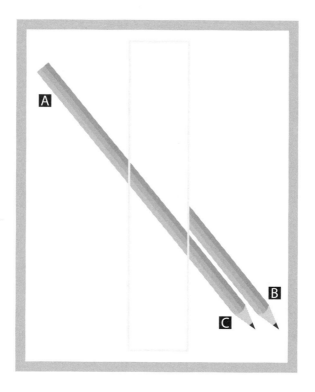

SHIFTY EYES

If you let your eyes roam around this image, you may see the shapes appear to move.

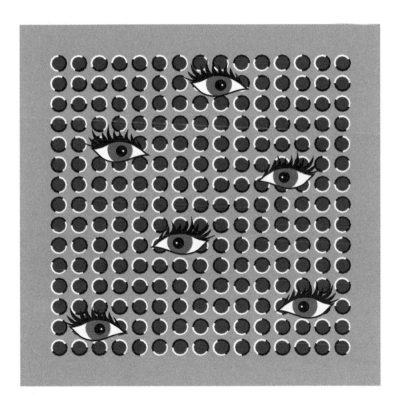

STRANGE FRUIT

You won't find this strange fruit at your local market.

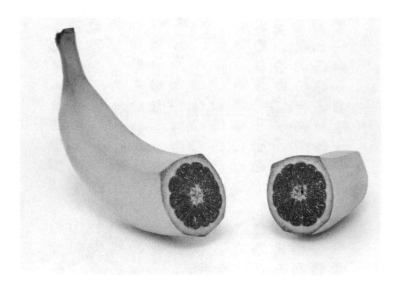

DIZZYING WHEELS

Look closely—but not too closely—as the wheels seem
to swirl around. Are you dizzy yet?

INFINITE FRAMES

These frames seem to repeat endlessly.

BARCODE

Though there appear to be 2 different shades of gray bars, it's just an illusion—they are identical shades of gray.

HERING ILLUSION

Are the vertical lines below straight and parallel, or bowed out in the middle? As you can see on the next page, the vertical lines are perfectly straight and parallel. The background pattern makes them seem bowed. This is called the Hering illusion.

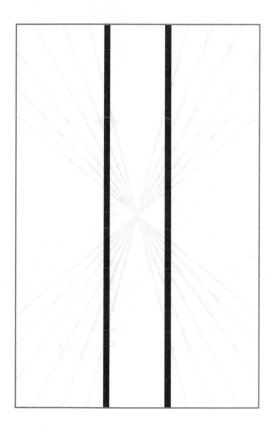

DEPTH PERCEPTION

With creative manipulation of perspective, this image gives the illusion of 3-dimensional depth.

ARROW LINES

Which center line is longer, the one between the arrows pointing in (top), or the one between the arrows pointing out (bottom)? Turn the page to find out.

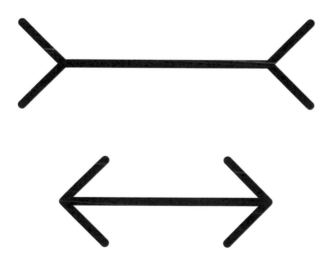

Answer on page 58.

ARROW LINES

They are the same length.

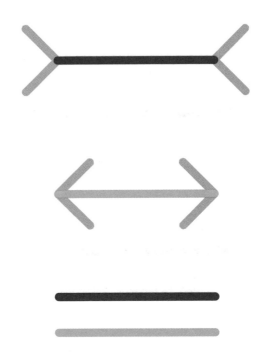

HEXAGON SWIRLS

Gaze at this illusion. Do you see the colorful discs within the hexagon swirl around?

WHALE TAIL

By shifting some lines in this square, it appears that a whale's tail is rising from within.

PARALLELOGRAM

Which is the longer line, A or B? Flip to the following page to find out.

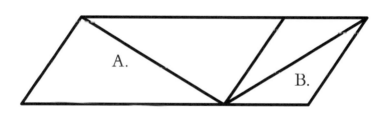

Answer on page 62.

PARALLELOGRAM

They are both the same length.

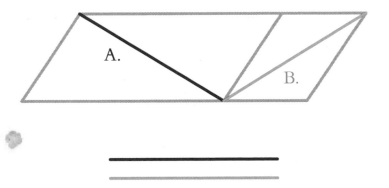

BEETLE BOARD

Which square on the checkerboard is lighter, the one with the red beetle or the one with the green beetle?

Answer on page 244.

CORAL CAMO

Optical illusions occur in nature. Animals use camouflage to hide in plain sight. Can you spot the camouflaged sea creature in this coral?

SOMETHING FISHY

There's something fishy going on in this image—the fish appear to move! The light and dark edges contribute to the apparent lateral movement.

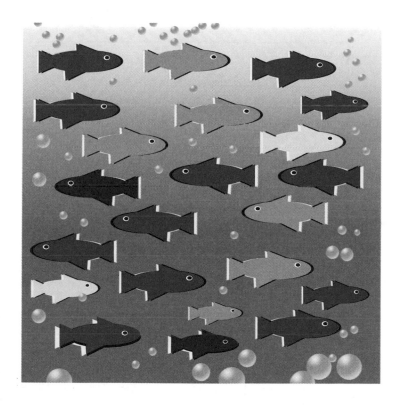

DISTORTED SQUARES?

While the red squares on this page look distorted, you can see from the next page that they are not.

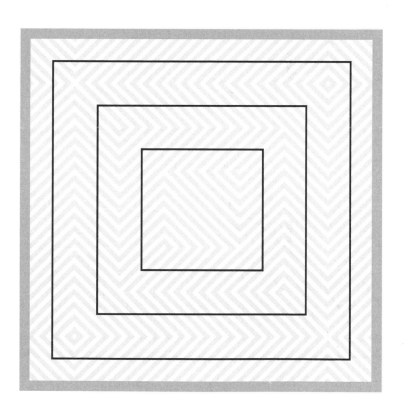

DEVIL'S FORK

What's wrong with this fork?

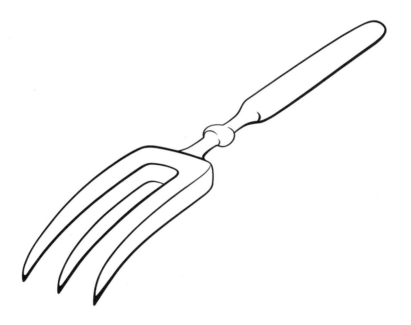

Answer on page 244.

SUSPENDED SLICES

These apple slices and knife appear to be suspended in mid-air, but it's just an illusion.

SHADES OF GRAY

Although there appear to be multiple shades of gray used in this image, you can see on the next page that they are the same shade. The gray squares seem darker or lighter depending on the colors surrounding them.

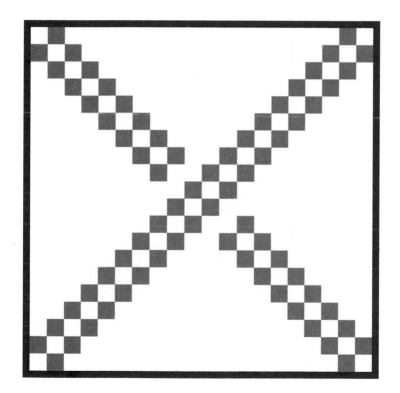

OPEN DOORS

While the open doors in this image seem realistic, there is no way they could all exist in the real world.

MISSHAPEN SHAPES

The brain interprets the red shapes in the foreground incorrectly in this case of perception distortion. The red shapes get contrasted to the blue lines in the background, making the red shapes appear distorted.

WARPED LINES?

Do these horizontal red lines warp in the center, or are they straight?

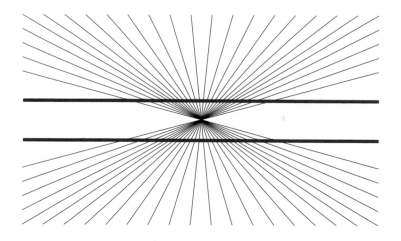

Answer on page 244.

FOOTPRINT IN THE SAND

Do you think this footprint is rising up out of the sand? Think again. This is actually an imprint, though it appears otherwise.

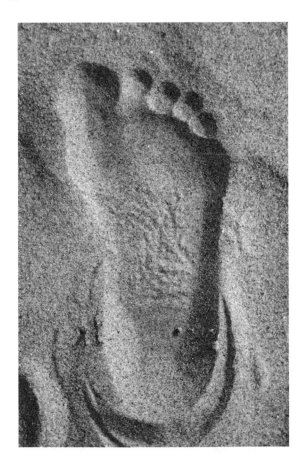

IMPOSSIBLE FIGURE

This figure is easy to draw, but impossible to make. That's because it's an impossible figure that can only appear in 2 dimensions.

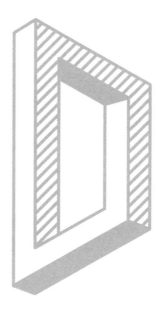

BLOOMING GREENS

Watch as the green petals seem to bloom before your eyes. The petals appear to pulsate and expand outward from the center.

PENCIL HEIGHT

Which is the taller pencil? While the pencil on the right seems taller in this image, you can see on the next page that both pencils are the same height.

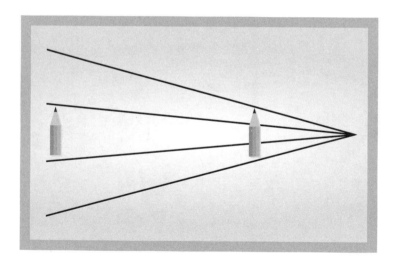

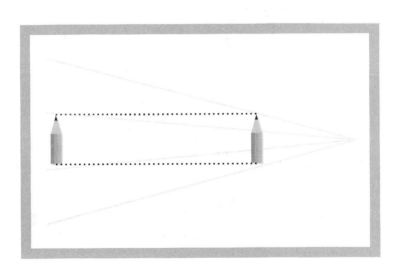

AMAZON LEAF TOAD

Can you find the toad camouflaged in this photograph?

IMPOSSIBLE BOX

At first glance, this box may appear normal, but a closer look reveals that this object is impossible to create. Impossible objects can only exist in 2 dimensions.

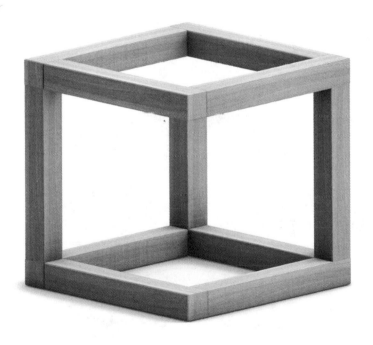

UNDER THE ROOF

What do you see under the roof—a vase or faces? This take on the classic Rubin's vase illusion creates multiple perceptions. The image can be perceived as a vase or as the profiles of 2 faces.

PULL UP A CHAIR

Good luck trying to sit on this wall chair! In this photo, the chair on the wall seems to defy the laws of gravity.

UP OR DOWN?

Are these tiles facing up or down? Also, study the top and bottom rows. The tiles aren't completely outlined; but, because the middle tiles are complete, your mind fills in the gaps.

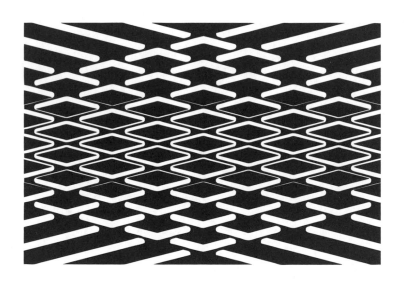

DOUBLE T

This figure defies the rules of space. Do your eyes switch between 2 perspectives—the right side up T and the upside down T? That's because this is an impossible figure.

WHICH WINDOW?

Which is the larger window? While the window on the
right looks larger, you can see on the following page that
the windows are the same size.

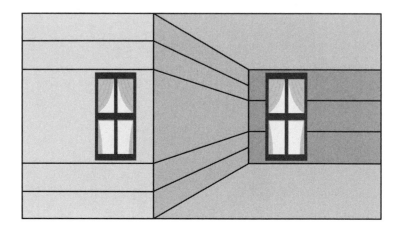

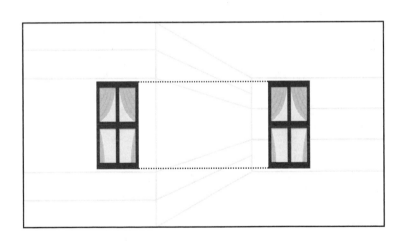

POTEMKIN STAIRS

The Potemkin Stairs in Odessa, Ukraine, give the illusion of greater depth because the stairs are much wider at the bottom than at the top.

TWO VIEWS

What do you see in this illusion—a dog or cats?

CUBE CONUNDRUM

What's wrong with this cube?

Answer on page 244.

CURVED LINES?

Do the blue lines curve inward, or are they straight?

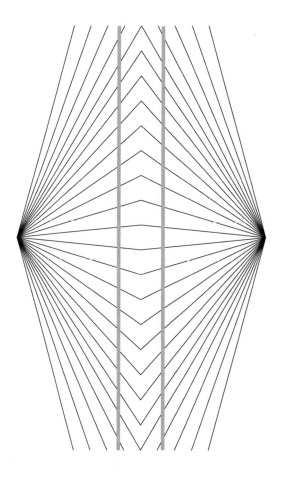

Answer on page 244.

PICTURE PERFECT ILLUSION

There's something strange about this picture. At first glance, it seems this woman is standing upright. But a closer look reveals that she is actually resting with her back on the ground.

MEN IN MOTION

Do these rows of men seem to shift? The black and white sides of the men contribute to the illusion of lateral motion.

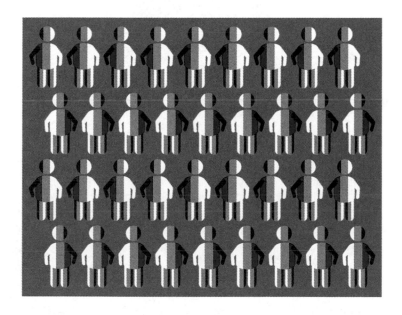

OP ART STAR

Do parts of this image seem to swell up off the page? Don't be fooled by this star—its lines only give the impression of depth.

BALANCING ACT

It looks like these chairs are doing the impossible—balancing. The key word here is "impossible." This is just a clever photograph.

WHAT DO YOU SEE?

Do you notice anything unusual about this tree trunk?
Look closely and you'll see the profiles of 2 faces.

SNAKES IN THE GRASS

If you let your eyes dart around this image, you may notice the snakes appear to slither.

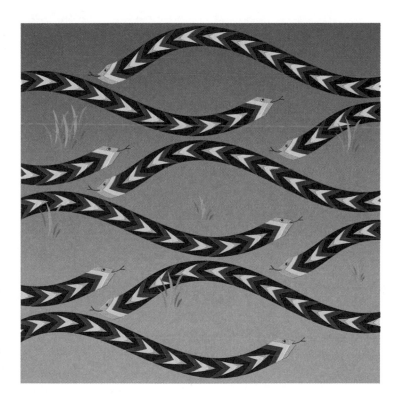

KEY SHADOW

How can this key create this shadow? It can't. This is just an illusion.

GEARS IN MOTION

When viewed with your peripheral vision, you may notice these colorful gears seem to rotate before your eyes.

WARPED GRID

With the help of some carefully placed white squares, it appears that a circle is rising from this grid. The reality is that a circlular shape is only suggested. Your mind fills in the gaps.

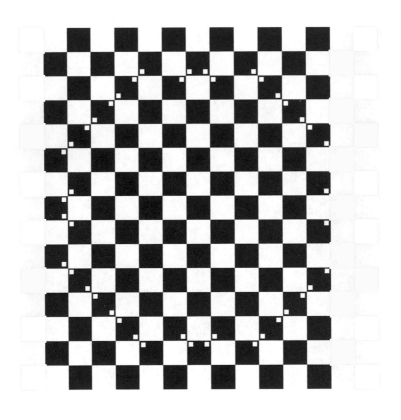

HULA GIRL

There are 2 errors hidden in the image of the hula girl. Can you spot them both?

Answers on page 244.

LINKED TRIANGLES

What's wrong with these linked triangles? They can't exist in 3 dimensions.

SNAKE EYE

Stare at the tubes surrounding the snake eye as they spin.

FLOWER POWER

These flowers seem to have the power to expand and bloom before your eyes.

LOOK AT IT THIS WAY

If this horse seems to have a few human characteristics, it's no coincidence. Flip this page over and find out why!

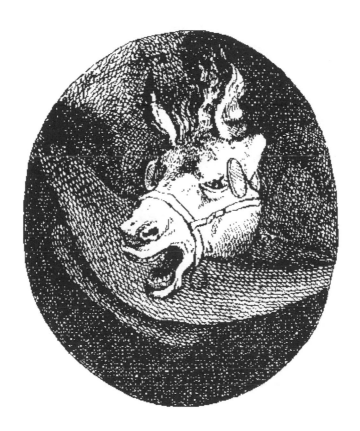

UNDER CONSTRUCTION

This construction would be impossible to create.

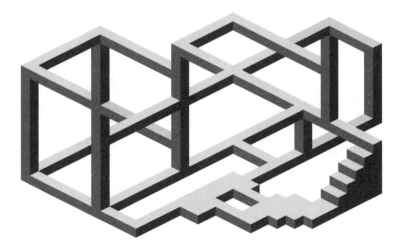

COLORED IN?

Although the continents and surrounding water appear to be shaded in (with colors orange and blue, respectively), they are in fact uniformly white! The color sensation is caused by the contrasting color outlines.

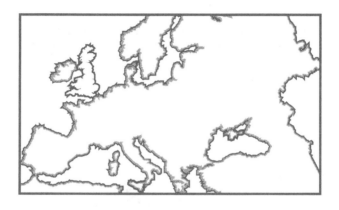

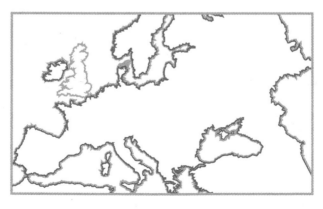

BEYOND GRAVITY

No, this dancer isn't really suspended in mid-air. This is a creative photo that has been manipulated.

CATCHING SOME Zs

Someone isn't finding this Sunday's sermon all that interesting. In fact, it's put him to sleep. Can you find the snoozing worshiper?

Answer on page 244.

PSYCHEDELIC SPINS

Shift your eyes around this psychedelic pattern and the static rings may appear to spin.

X MARKS THE SPOT

Which square with an X is darker?

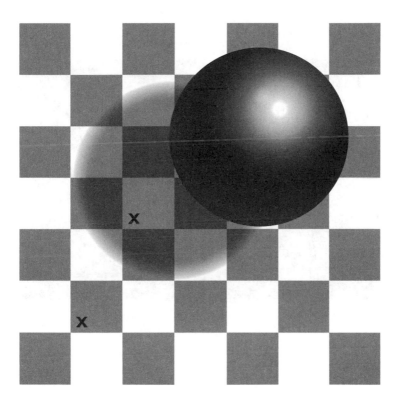

Answer on page 245.

TWO-WAY TUNNEL

Do you see how the green and black arrows forming
this tunnel point in opposite directions?

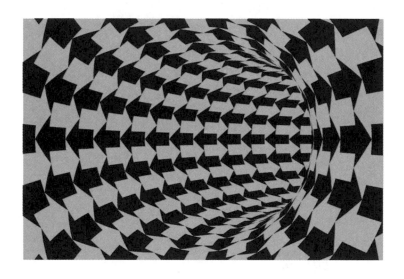

ARROW WEB

Shade in some of the arrows so that each arrow in the grid points to exactly one shaded arrow.

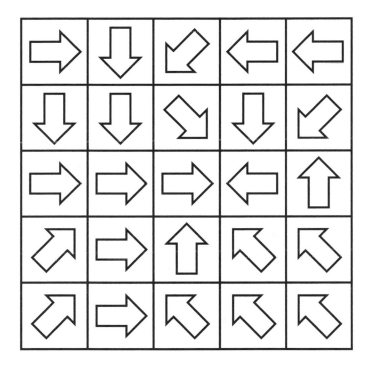

Answer on page 245.

ILLUSORY CONTOURS

Do you see a triangle floating above another triangle?
The shape you see is an illusion created by the shaded
points and missing parts of the background triangle.

DRIFTING SPHERES

Move your eyes around this image and the spheres may appear to move.

FLASHING CIRCLES

Take a look at this grid. What happens to the white circles? They should turn to gray.

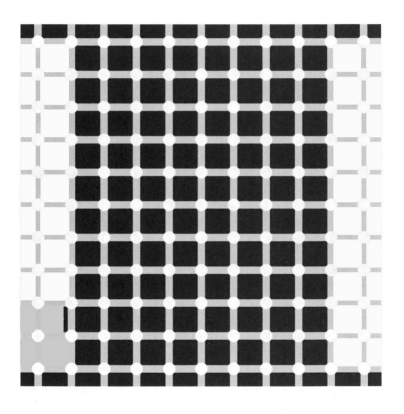

MONKEY BUSINESS

This is clearly a picture of a monkey, wouldn't you agree? But maybe there's something more going on here. Maybe if you turn the page upside down, you'll be facing something unexpected.

SNAPSHOT SPINNERS

Check out the seemingly spinning wheels in this snapshot.

REVERSED REFLECTION

Which is the sky and which is the water? It's hard to tell at first, but this photo is reversed so the reflection of the water is on top and the sky is on the bottom.

IDENTITY PARADE

Four mugshots accidentally got shredded, and Officer Burns is trying to straighten them out. Currently, only one facial feature in each row is in its correct place. Officer Burns knows that:

1. C's nose is one place to the left of D's mouth.
2. C's eyes are one place to the right of C's hair.
3. B's nose is not next to C's nose.
4. A's eyes are 2 places to the left of A's mouth.
5. C's eyes are not next to A's eyes.
6. D's hair is one place to the right of B's nose.

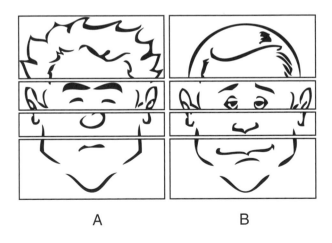

A   B

Can you find the correct hair, eyes, nose, and mouth for each person?

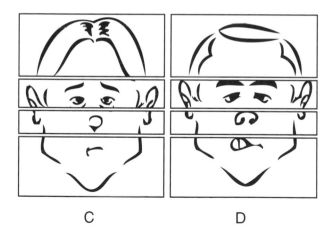

C   D

Answer on page 245.

DANCING DRAGONFLIES

Gaze at this illusion and watch the dragonflies seemingly dance around.

AMBIGRAM

Turn this page upside down. What do you notice?
The word England can be read both ways.

ENGLAND

LADYBUGS

The dots in the background appear to move, but they are really stuck on the page.

SQUARE AREA

If the area of the big square is 1, what is the area of the small square in the middle?

A. ¹⁄₄
B. ¹⁄₅
C. ¹⁄₆
D. ¹⁄₇

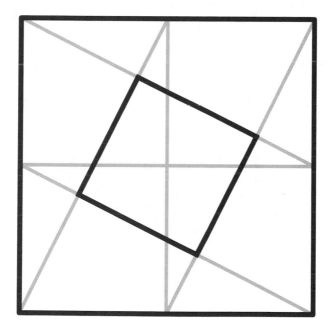

Answer on page 245.

YIN-YANG ILLUSION

Don't fall for this illusion—the wheels only seem to spin.

FUNNY BUNNIES

Something's wrong with the math here. There are 3 bunnies, but only 3 ears. Yet this image seems on the up-and-up. At closer study, the trick becomes evident—these bunnies are sharing ears.

ROTATING CATS

Don't be fooled by this motion illusion. The cats only appear to rotate.

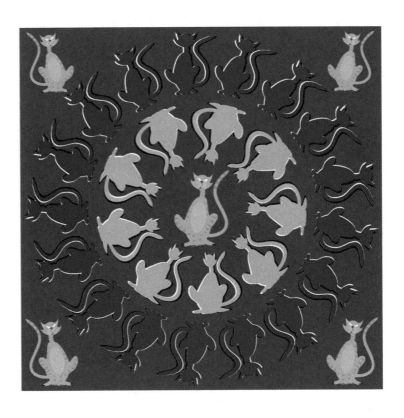

LINGERING IMAGE

We have a task for you: Stare at this skull for 30 seconds. Then, look at a white sheet of paper. What do you see?

Answer on page 246.

PLUGGED IN

Watch these plugged in wheels spin.

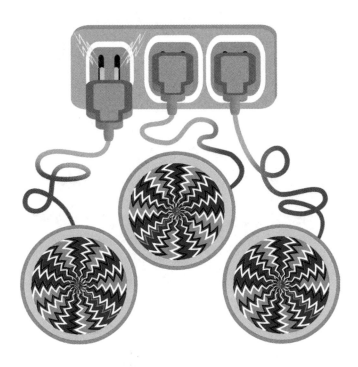

MISSING Fs

How many times does the letter F appear in the sentence below?

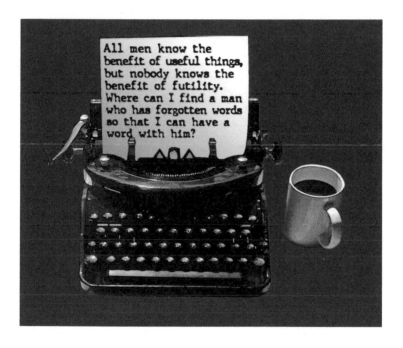

Answer on page 246.

A PUZZLING PERSPECTIVE

Which of the 3 men depicted in the drawing below is the tallest?

Answer on page 246.

CRYSTAL BALL

Look into this ball of glass and you'll see an upside down world. This illusion of refraction occurs because light passes through the glass ball and flips the image upside down.

PSYCHEDELIC PULSE

Gaze at this psychedelic image and you might see the waves of colors pulsing.

STAR CONTRAST

Are the octagons within the Yin-Yang symbol below the same color?

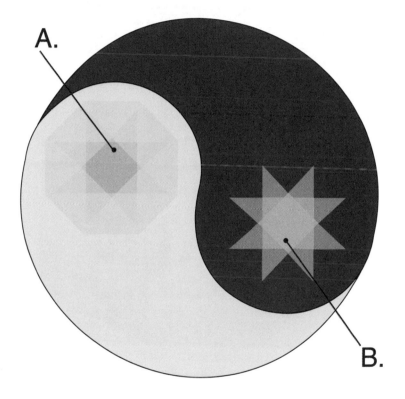

Answer on page 246.

IMPOSSIBLE TOY

You would not find this impossible design at your local toy store.

BIRDHOUSE

Begin by looking at this puzzle at a normal reading distance. Slowly, move the page closer to your face. As you do, you'll see the bird find its way home.

AROUND AND AROUND

Stare at this image and watch the blue shapes appear to swirl around.

STRAIGHT LINES

Do the red lines passing through the circle appear to bend? They are perfectly straight—this is an illusion caused by the rings the red lines pass through.

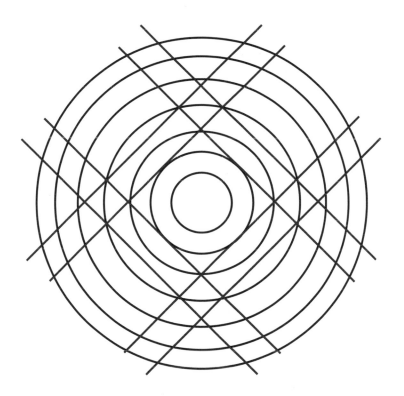

GRAY SHADES

Take a look at this image—seems like there are multiple shades of gray, right? Actually, there are only 2 shades used. Colors seem darker or lighter depending on the colors they are surrounded by.

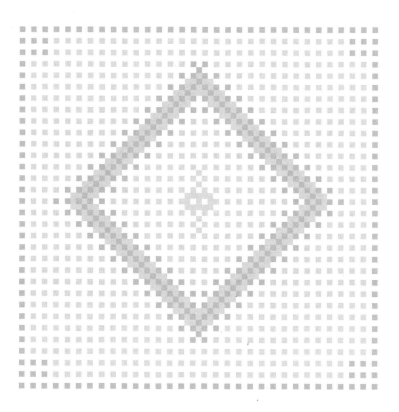

A BOX OF ILLUSIONS

Though static on the page, the zigzag wheels on this box seem to spin.

CLOWNING AROUND

This clown's wig appears to grow, but it's just an illusion.

DOUBLE V

Look at the Vs. Are they the same color?

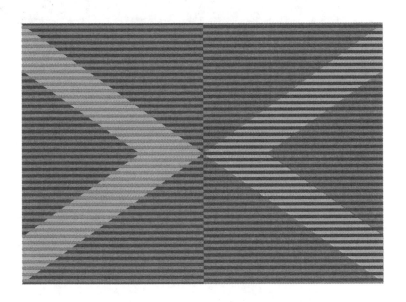

Answer on page 247.

ROLL THE DICE

Study the dice—which red dot is bigger?

Answer on page 247.

IMPOSSIBLE!

This impossible structure cannot exist in the 3-dimensional world. Look how the joints meet—no real figure can have sides that meet in such a way.

WHICH WAY?

Which way are the arrows pointing? It depends on if you're looking at the colored arrows or white arrows.

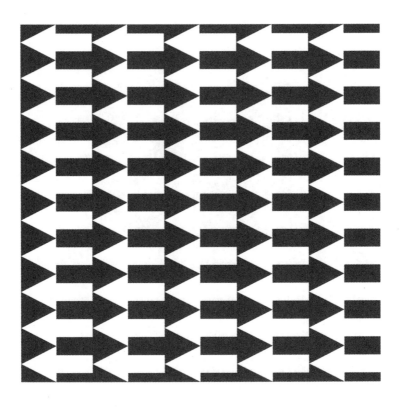

TRICKY TABLES

Do these tabletops have the same length and width?

Answer on page 247.

THREE RINGS

The colors used in these intertwined rings give the illusion of movement.

FRONT/BACK

Imagine you are driving and you see the reflection of this car in your rearview mirror. Can you read the message on the hood? What does it say? See the next page to find out.

Answer on page 150.

FRONT/BACK

This is an ambigram. Read one way, the letters read "front"; read another, they read "back."

FRONT

BACK

UPSIDE DOWN SMILE

Like many other illusions, this image gives you one thing while keeping another out of sight. At least sight in the sense of how we're accustomed to looking at things. Turn this page upside down, and you'll turn those grins around as well.

ON ROTATION

Stare at these static spirals—do they appear to rotate?

YOUNG OR OLD?

Are the old, ugly woman on the left and the beautiful, young princess on the right one and the same? Turn this page upside down to find out.

BOOKENDS

Which line, A or B, is connected to C?

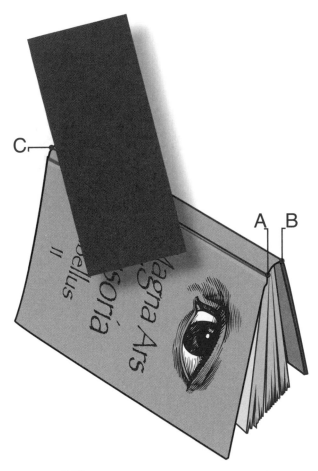

Answer on page 247.

FERRIS WHEEL

You don't need to leave home to take a trip on this Ferris wheel! Just concentrate on this illusion and watch the wheel spin.

CHARGED-UP ZIGZAGS

These charged-up zigzags seem to swirl.

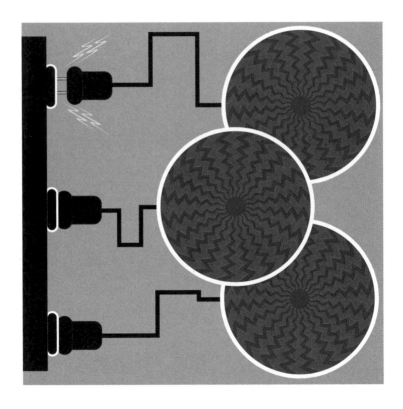

FLOWER GROWTH

Which of these flowers has the longest stem?

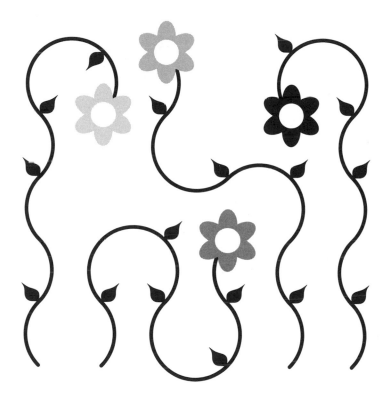

Answer on page 248.

FIND THE LOVERS

Ah, young love. So many times it has to stay hidden. In this case, the clandestine affair is literal. Find the kissing couple in the illustration below.

Answer on page 248.

HAPPY HEARTS

These happy hearts seem to swirl, but it's just an illusion.

SQUARE HOLDINGS

Which of the 2 interior squares are exactly the same?

Answer on page 248.

SQUARES WITHIN SQUARES

The squares fold in on themselves until collapsing at the center.

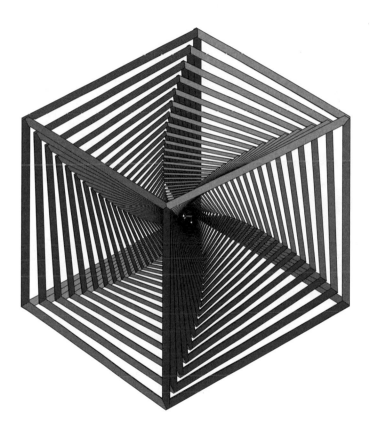

CIRCULAR REASONING

Which interior blue circle is smaller, the one on the left or the one on the right?

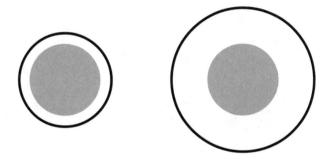

Answer on page 248.

JAGGED LINES

Try to follow the black and white lines in this image. Having trouble? The lines aren't continuous—they only appear to be due to a trick of the shapes and colors.

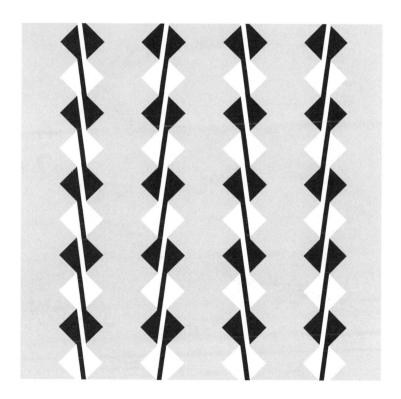

PUZZLING PLATES

Don't be fooled here—these spinning plates only give the illusion of movement.

EBBINGHAUS ILLUSION

While the center blue circle on the left looks smaller than the blue circle on the right, they are the same size. The Ebbinghaus illusion is a relative size perception illusion. How we perceive the size of the center blue circles is influenced by the size of the surrounding circles.

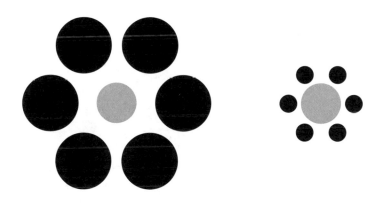

UP IN SMOKE

There's a thief in this man's midst—and he's stolen his best cigars! See if you can focus your visual acuity and spot the cigar thief.

Answer on page 249.

STRANDS OF BEADS

As you look at this image, do you see the strands of beads seem to sway?

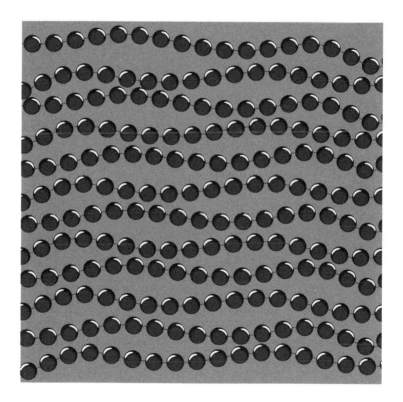

INTERRUPTED LINES

Which of the lines above is extended below?

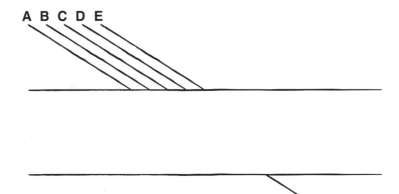

Answer on page 249.

ROTATING ZIGZAGS

Try to maintain your perspective while gazing at these seemingly rotating zigzags.

IMPOSSIBLE PERCH

What's wrong with this drawing?

Answer on page 249.

SAIL ON BY

It's smooth sailing for these boats. Do you notice how these rows of sailboats seem to move?

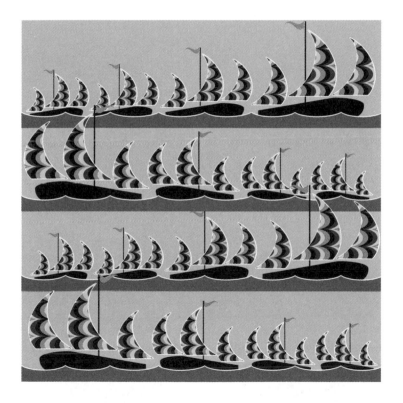

SPIRAL WHEELS

No, these spiral wheels aren't actually moving—though they sure seem like they are!

A SHADY SHAPE

Our brains use clues like shading to turn 2-D images like this into something that looks 3-D. Based on our past experiences with shading, our brains can jump to the incorrect assumption that this shape has depth.

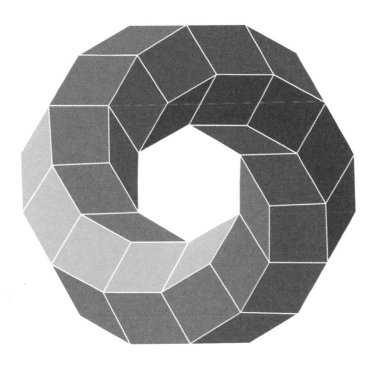

DRAWING THE LINE

Believe it or not, but hidden in this line illustration is a cat. Can you pinpoint Kitty's secret location?

Answer on page 249.

LOOK THIS WAY

Do you see how the eyes in this illusion appear to move from side to side?

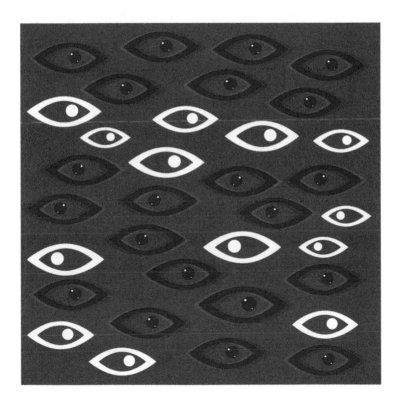

IMPOSSIBLE SHAPE

Here is another shape that, while looking correct at first glance, is actually impossible to create.

90 DEGREES

How many 90-degree angles are hidden in this image?

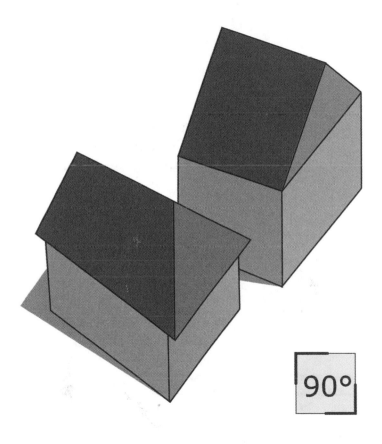

90°

Answer on page 250.

REVERSIBLE CHIMNEYS

You probably see 2 chimney tops in this image—one in the upper part and another in the lower part. Each apparent chimney leads downward. This equivocal illusion has more than one single interpretation.

BLOOMING FLOWER

Watch as the triangular petals of this flower seem to expand outward.

ORANGE SWIRLS

Stare at these orange shapes long enough and they appear to swirl.

PYRAMID LINES

Are lines A and B the same length?

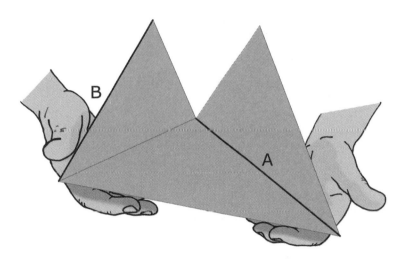

Answer on page 250.

STRAW ALIGNMENT

At first sight, it seems that all the red lines on the left straw can be continued into the green and orange lines on the middle and right straws. Is that possible?

Answer on page 250.

SHIFTING SQUARES

Sure, these squares are locked into their positions on the page, but that doesn't stop them from at least appearing to shift from dark to light!

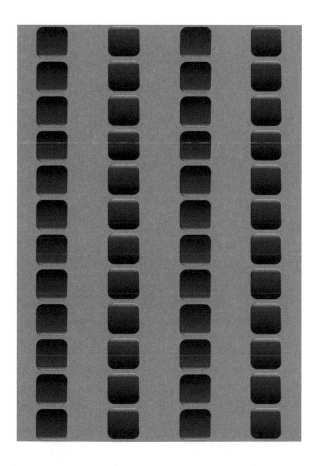

DEVILISH DOGS

There may be the same number of dog heads and dog tails, but there's something strange about this seamless pattern of dogs. The heads and tails don't match up!

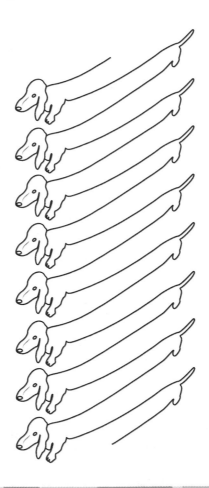

SCHOLARS

Which of the 3 men depicted is the tallest?

Answer on page 251.

SPIRAL DESIGN

Both statues below (A and B) contain spiral designs.
Statue B is a mirror image of A yet something is wrong.
Can you spot the difference between the 2 statues?

A.

B.

Answer on page 251.

HEART AND SOUL

The pink hearts in the top right and bottom left squares are darker than the other 2 hearts, right? Wrong! All 4 hearts are identical in color.

BOW BONANZA

The gold bows seem to expand out from the center, but this is just an illusion.

FRACTURED LETTER

What letter do you see here?

Answer on page 251.

CIRCULAR RISING

By readjusting some lines in this pattern, it appears that a circle is rising from within.

SPIN CYCLE

Sweep your eyes around this image. Do you notice how the brightly colored zigzag wheels seem to spin?

GET TO THE POINT

Though this shape appears to be coming off the page, it's just an illusion. Thanks to perspective and space manipulation, the focal point appears to be on the rise, or in retreat, depending on how you look at it.

DUCK OR RABBIT?

In this classic illusion, the image can easily be 2 different things. Here, you have a long-billed duck. But look at it from another perspective, and watch that bill turn into ears, and that duck look more and more like a rabbit.

SEAMLESS CUBES

The arrangement and shading of these stacked cubes gives the illusion of depth where there is none.

TRICKY TERRACE

Which direction is this man facing?

Answer on page 252.

SAND DUNE DISGUISE

What animal is hidden in these sand dunes?

Answer on page 252.

A STORMY ILLUSION

Let your eyes bolt around this stormy image. Not only do the lightning bolts seem to have depth—they also seem to move!

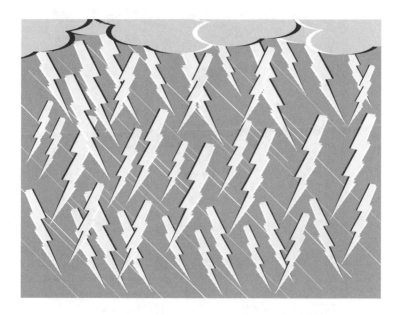

DOUBLE FACE

How many faces do you see here—2 or 3? This kind of illusion, known as an "undecidable image," has been around since ancient times!

Answer on page 252.

THE BLUES

Look at the 2 stars. Are they the same shade of blue?

Answer on page 253.

A PIECE OF CAKE

When you look at this ambiguous drawing, you may
see a cake with a piece cut out. Turn the drawing upside
down and you suddenly see a single piece of cake on a
plate. In this equivocal illusion, the drawing has more
than one interpretation.

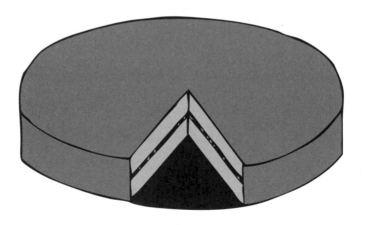

PEOPLE PATTERN

Don't be fooled by the people in this pattern. They only seem to roll back and forth.

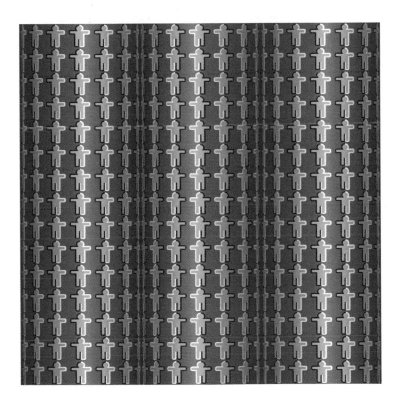

DUCK COLOR

Recover the white plumage color of the duck on page 203! To restore the color balance, stare at the X in the diagram below for 20 seconds, then shift your gaze over to the duck, specifically to the O in the diagram.

THE PULSE

Take a quick glance and you'll see something unusual with this picture—the lines appear to pulse. This is an illusion of design, created by how the lines are laid out.

OUCHI ILLUSION

This variation on the Ouchi illusion demonstrates a brilliant contrast effect. As you stare at the image, the circle in the foreground will separate from the background and shimmer.

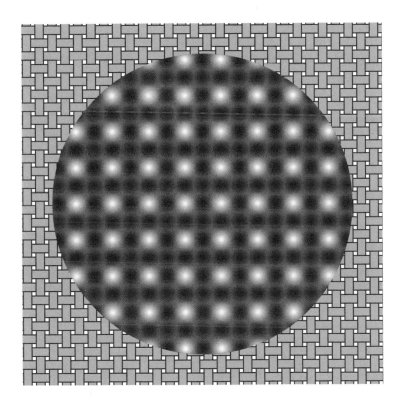

DISTORTED SQUARES

Which of the squares below is actually a proper, real square, A or B?

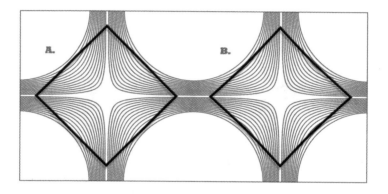

Answer on page 253.

IMPOSSIBLE OBJECT

At first the object below may appear normal, but closer inspection reveals that this 2-dimensional object cannot exist in our 3-dimensional world.

FADE TO WHITE

Concentrate on the black circle in the center. Hold your focus and watch the surrounding gray disappear.

FLOWER GROWTH

Which of these flowers has the longest stem?

Answer on page 253.

RAINBOW BRIGHT

The colors in the rainbow on this page have completely faded. To brighten it back up, stare at the white dot in the rainbow on the next page for 20 seconds, then shift your gaze back to the rainbow below. This illusion is based on color adaptation and afterimage effect.

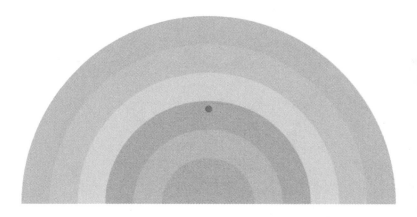

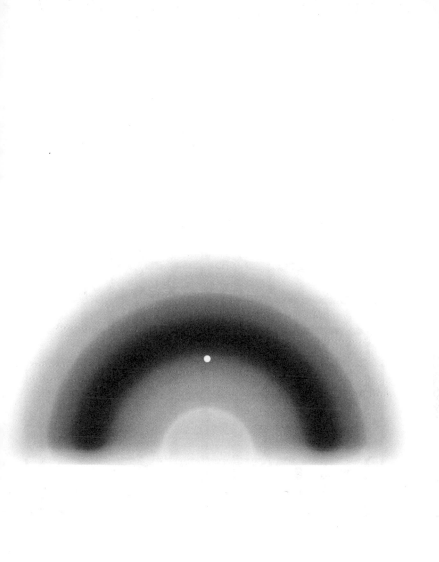

SWOLLEN ILLUSION

Take a good look at this image—not only does the center appear to extend outward, but something else is going on as well. After only a few seconds, white dots should form in the black lines. This is an afterimage effect.

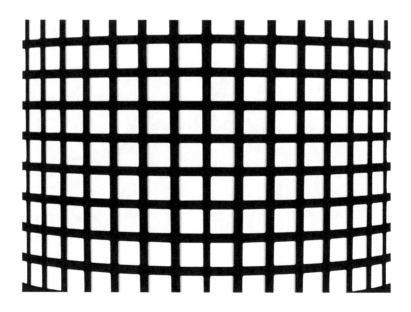

PUZZLE PIECES

Are these 2 puzzle pieces the same color?

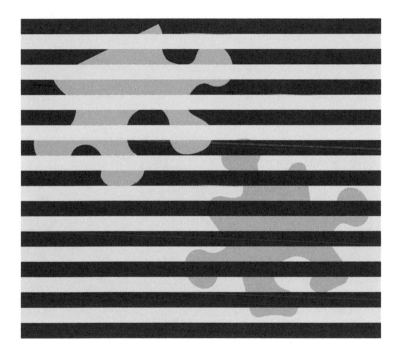

Answer on page 254.

SOFA STRIPES

Which color stripe is an exact match for stripe A—stripe B or stripe C?

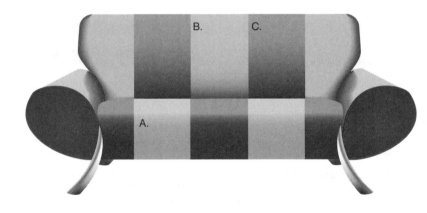

Answer on page 254.

UNREAL TRIANGLE

This interlocking triangle, no matter how you look at it, cannot exist in the real world.

AROUND IN CIRCLES

Which of the 4 lines is the longest?

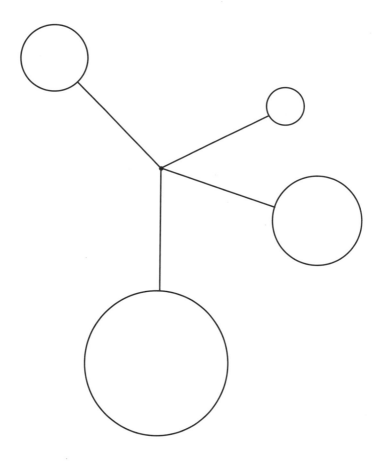

Answer on page 254.

HANDS HOLDING

The triangle below is not a triangle at all. The shape you see is an illusion created by the 3 hands and the shaded points. The white is the exact same color as the background.

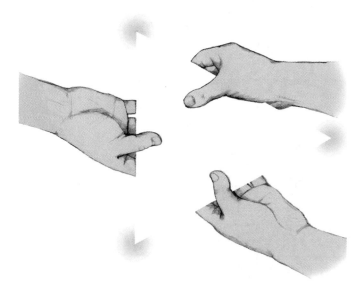

PUZZLING PINWHEELS

Try to keep your perspective while gazing at these puzzling pinwheels.

CHOPPER LINES

Which line is longer, red or blue?

Answer on page 254.

CHEESE VISION

Which piece of cheese (A, B, or C) is cut from the semicircle below?

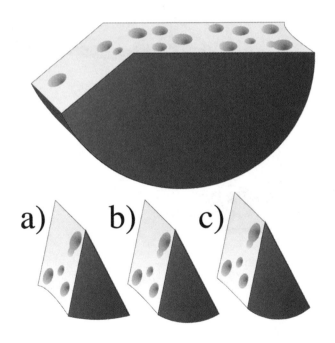

a)   b)   c)

Answer on page 255.

RECORD PLAYER

Check out the circle below; if you stare at it long enough, it will appear to spin, like a record.

HOLE IN ONE

This illusion is the result of some creative photography.

SPLIT LINES

Which piece completes the line, the top one or the bottom one?

Answer on page 255.

CAFÉ TILES

These rows of tiles look uneven, but they're perfectly straight. They appear to run at angles due to the off-center design of the yellow and blue tiles. This distortion was discovered on the tiled wall of a café in England.

HOW MANY ARROWS?

How many arrows can you see? Are you sure? Count them again.

Answer on page 255.

PINSTRIPES

Which is darker—the blue color in the inner square or
the blue color in the outer square?

Answer on page 255.

GET SOME PERSPECTIVE

This what happens when perspective goes awry—this block illustration has no vanishing point, and thus no clear perspective.

COPYRIGHTS

Are each pair of letters in these typographical symbols the same size, or are they different?

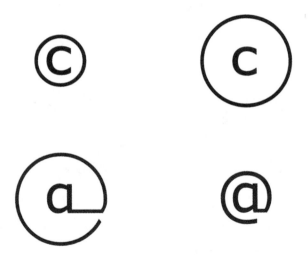

Answer on page 255.

CIRCULAR MOTION

Move your head back and forth while focusing on these circles. They appear to shift with your movements.

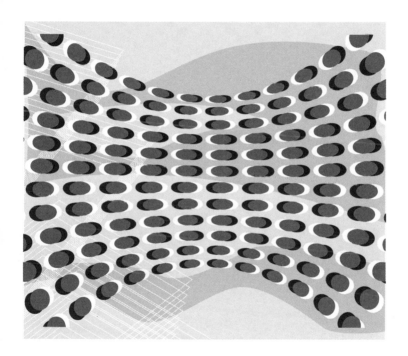

ANOTHER DIMENSION

The box appears to have depth; the circle inside it appears to have shape. But, this is only a manipulation of space and dimension!

OUTFOXED

Hidden in this tranquil scene is an outline of a fox. Can you find it?

Answer on page 256.

COLUMN CONFUSION

These columns seem to bend and bow, but do they really? Nope, these columns are completely straight and parallel to each other. It's the slanted lines inside the columns that trick our eyes.

INVISIBLE MAN

There's no explaining this one. This altered image leaves no trace of a man but his shadow and his shoes.

THAT'S IMPOSSIBLE!

This figure cannot exist in the 3-dimensional world.

WINDING ABYSS

Stare deeply into this image; the circles appear to spiral in toward the middle, even though they remain in straight rows.

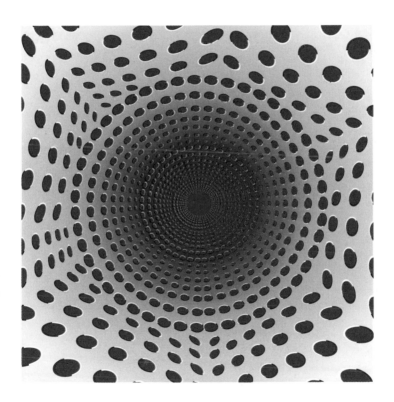

ALIEN INVADERS

These alien invaders are tough to shoot. They seem to be moving from side to side.

CONVERGENT ALIGNMENTS

Do the 2 alignments of black and white segments move toward one another at the top? Or are they parallel?

Answer on page 256.

HEIGHT TIMES WIDTH

Which is wider, the H or the W?

Answer on page 256.

TWIRLING TILES

Keep your eyes moving around this image to see the twirling effect of the tiles.

TOTALLY CUBULAR!

What do you see here? Cubes? Rectangles? The number 6? The number 9?

HOW MANY TRIANGLES?

Triangles are pointed in every direction. How many can you count?

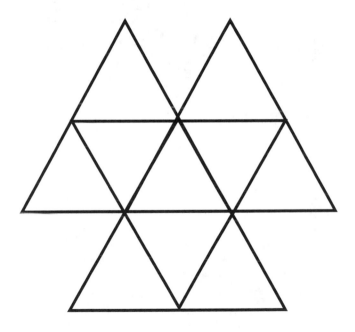

Answer on page 256.

SPINNING ZIG, TURNING ZAG

These static shapes are locked into their positions on the page, but that doesn't stop them from at least appearing to move!

IMPOSSIBLE OR NOT?

Which of these figures is *not* an impossible shape?

Answer on page 256.

ANSWER KEY

BEETLE BOARD
(page 63)

Both squares are
the same shade.

CURVED LINES?
(page 91)

The blue lines are straight.

DEVIL'S FORK
(page 68)

The fork appears
to have 2 tines that
mysteriously transform
into 3 tines.

HULA GIRL (page 101)

1. She has 2 right feet;
2. She has 6 fingers on
her left hand (counting
the concealed thumb)

WARPED LINES?
(page 74)

The black background
lines make the red lines
appear to warp, but they
are straight.

CATCHING SOME Zs
(page 109)

CUBE CONUNDRUM
(page 90)

It's an impossible figure.

ANSWER KEY

X MARKS THE SPOT (page 111)

They are the same. This is an effect of shadow and surrounding colors. The X shaded by the ball appears lighter, but only because the surrounding squares are darker, due to the shadow cast over them.

ARROW WEB (page 113)

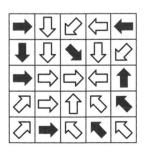

IDENTITY PARADE (pages 120–121)

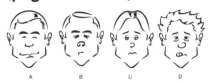

SQUARE AREA (page 125)

B. $\frac{1}{5}$

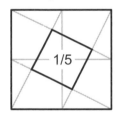

ANSWER KEY

LINGERING IMAGE (page 129)

The skull appears on the sheet of paper, only the blacks and whites are reversed.

MISSING Fs (page 131)

Most people count 6 Fs, but there are actually 8! It's easy to glaze over the Fs in the preposition of— words such as "and," "from," and "of" are processed uncon- sciously by our mind.

A PUZZLING PERSPECTIVE (page 132)

The 3 men are all the same size. The perspective lines drawn behind the men trick us into thinking the top man is farther away and therefore the tallest. This illusion suggests we judge size based on its background.

STAR CONTRAST (page 135)
Yes.

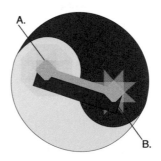

ANSWER KEY

DOUBLE V
(page 143)

Yes, they are the same color. Both are influenced by the surrounding colors.

ROLL THE DICE
(page 144)

Even though the red dot on the farther die seems much larger, it is the exact same size as the red dot on the closer die. The illusion is a trick of perception.

TRICKY TABLES
(page 147)

Yes. Trace them if you're not convinced!

BOOKENDS
(page 154)

ANSWER KEY

FLOWER GROWTH
(page 157)

SQUARE HOLDINGS
(page 160)

FIND THE LOVERS
(page 158)

CIRCULAR REASONING
(page 162)

They are the same size.

ANSWER KEY

UP IN SMOKE
(page 166)

IMPOSSIBLE PERCH
(page 170)

The stairs, and the cat's perch upon them, are impossible. These stairs could not be built with raw materials.

INTERRUPTED LINES
(page 168)

Most people think that the answer is D, but A is the correct answer.

DRAWING THE LINE
(page 174)

ANSWER KEY

90 DEGREES
(page 177)

There are 8 angles. Most people locate 6, though there are 2 deceptive angles hidden between the houses. Some of the angles may not look like right angles, but this due to a trick of apparent perspective.

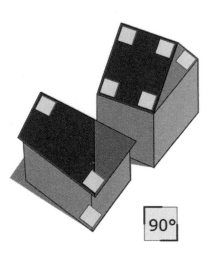

PYRAMID LINES
(page 181)

Yes.

STRAW ALIGNMENT
(page 182)

It is not possible. Only diagonal lines of the same color can be continuously linked together.

ANSWER KEY

SCHOLARS
(page 185)

The man in the foreground is actually 15 percent taller than the man in the background.

FRACTURED LETTER
(page 189)

SPIRAL DESIGN
(page 186)

The spiral in statue A is actually 2 spirals, while the spiral in B is 1 spiral.

A. 2 spirals

B. 1 double spiral

ANSWER KEY

TRICKY TERRACE (page 195)

There are 2 ways to perceive this image: from above (figure a.) or below (figure b.). These kinds of illusions are known as bistable figures.

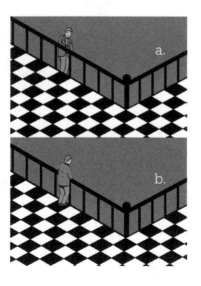

SAND DUNE DISGUISE (page 196)

An elephant is hidden on top.

DOUBLE FACE (page 198)

There are 3 faces— 2 looking directly at each other, and a third created by combining the 2 sides.

ANSWER KEY

THE BLUES (page 199)

Yes.

FLOWER GROWTH (page 209)

DISTORTED SQUARES (page 206)

Though most people say B, the answer is A! In cases of perception distortion, the brain interprets regular lines or shapes in the foreground incorrectly; those lines and shapes get contrasted to other lines and shapes in the background, making them appear distorted.

ANSWER KEY

PUZZLE PIECES
(page 213)

Yes, the puzzle pieces are the same color. The light colored bars crossing the top piece and the dark colored bars crossing the bottom piece impact how we see the identical color of both puzzle pieces.

SOFA STRIPES
(page 214)

Though it seems incredible, A and C are exactly alike. A color always seems brighter when surrounded by dark colors, and vice-versa.

AROUND IN CIRCLES
(page 216)

They're all equal length.

CHOPPER LINES
(page 219)

If you concentrate on the circle that surrounds the lines, the red line appears longer. But, if you concentrate on the helicopters instead, the blue line appears longer. The fact is that the blue line is the longest of the pair.

ANSWER KEY

CHEESE VISION
(page 220)

It would seem that B is that best fit, but the correct answer, when considering the exact angle and shape, is A.

SPLIT LINES
(page 223)

The top line.

HOW MANY ARROWS?
(page 225)

8.

PINSTRIPES
(page 226)

The blue color is the same throughout the figure. The black stripes in the inner square and the white stripes in the outer square influence the way we perceive the blue color.

COPYRIGHTS
(page 228)

They are all the same size. This illusion is known as an Ebbinghaus illusion.

ANSWER KEY

OUTFOXED
(page 231)

HEIGHT TIMES WIDTH (page 238)

Though it appears the H is wider, they are the same width.

HOW MANY TRIANGLES? (page 241)

There are 14 triangles.

CONVERGENT ALIGNMENTS (page 237)

The 2 vertical alignments of black and white segments are perfectly parallel to each other.

IMPOSSIBLE OR NOT? (page 243)

None of them. They are all impossible shapes.